VOLLEYBALL

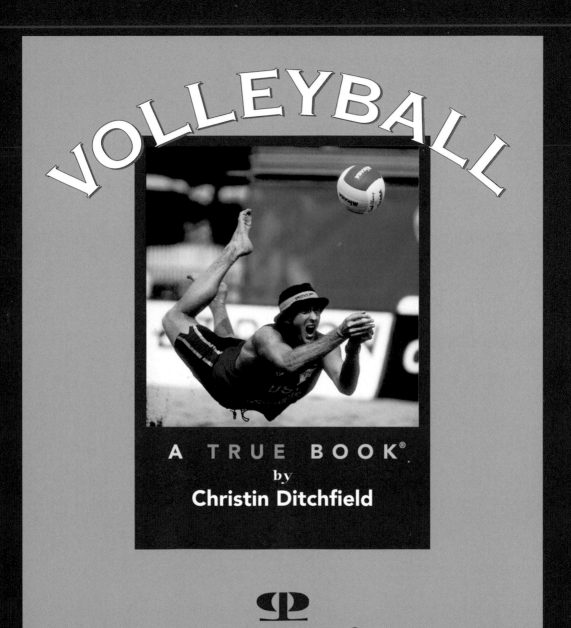

A TRUE BOOK®

by
Christin Ditchfield

ℂℙ

Children's Press®
A Division of Scholastic Inc.

New York Toronto London Auckland Sydney
Mexico City New Delhi Hong Kong
Danbury, Connecticut

An overhead view of
a high-school player
spiking the ball

Reading Consultant
Nanci R. Vargus, Ed.D.
Assistant Professor
Literacy Education
University of Indianapolis
Indianapolis, IN

Library of Congress Cataloging-in-Publication Data

Ditchfield, Christin.
    Volleyball / by Christin Ditchfield.
        p. cm. – (A true book)
Includes bibliographical references and index.
Summary: Explores the sport of volleyball, including its history, basic
rules, and terminology.
ISBN 0-516-22587-1 (lib bdg.)   0-516-26958-5 (pbk.)
1. Volleyball—Juvenile literature. [1. Volleyball.] I. Title. II. Series.
GV1015.34 .D58 2003
796.325—dc21
                                                                2001008379

Contents

A youth-league volleyball game

Mintonette

Every week, all over the world, more than 800 million people play volleyball. They don't need a lot of expensive equipment or special training to play. Teams of players just hit a lightweight ball back and forth across a net. People of all ages and fitness levels can enjoy this simple game. That's just what the inventor of volleyball had in mind.

In 1895, William G. Morgan was a **fitness** instructor at the Young Men's Christian Association (YMCA) in Holyoke, Massachusetts. Morgan wanted to find a way to help adults get more exercise—and have fun at the same time. He thought that basketball was too rough for people who were out of shape. It took too much physical energy.

William G. Morgan (left) invented volleyball while working at the YMCA in Holyoke, Massachusetts (right) in 1895.

Morgan decided to create his own game. He borrowed a net from a nearby tennis court and strung it up so that the top of it was at a height of 6.5 feet (2 meters)—just above the average man's head. He told his students to hit a ball across the net to each other, using only their arms or hands.

Morgan called the game "mintonette" because it reminded him of badminton. In badminton, players use light rackets to hit a small object across a high net. Mintonette quickly became a popular game.

One day, a college professor visited the YMCA to watch a

mintonette match. He saw how the players constantly "volleyed" the ball—hit the ball back and forth. The professor suggested that Morgan change the name of his game to "volleyball."

Women playing college volleyball in 1940

Through the YMCA, volleyball spread to athletic clubs and colleges across the United States. American soldiers introduced the game to Europe during World War I. An American **missionary** brought the game to Japan.

People everywhere loved to play volleyball. In 1928, sports officials formed the United States Volleyball Association to organize rules and competitions. In no time at all, volleyball

Today, volleyball is popular all over the world. These young men are playing volleyball in the Asian country of Myanmar.

clubs, **tournaments**, and organizations had sprung up all over the world. The simple little game was becoming a highly **competitive** sport.

The Basics

Like many other sports, volley-ball is played on a court shaped like a rectangle. A volleyball court measures 59 feet (18 m) long and 29.5 feet (9 m) wide. Painted **boundary** lines show where the court begins and ends. The long lines are called "sidelines." The shorter lines are called "end lines."

A center line runs across the middle of the court. A long net hangs above the center line. The net is 3 feet (1 m) tall and 32 feet (9.7 m) wide.

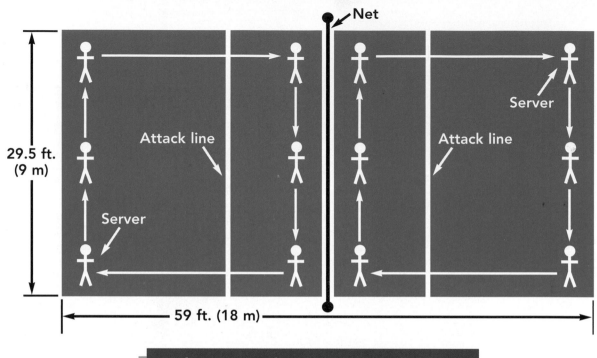

29.5 ft. (9 m)

Net

Server

Attack line

Attack line

Server

59 ft. (18 m)

"Attack lines" are painted on each side of the court, 9.8 feet (3 m) away from the net.

In a friendly game of volley-ball, there may be any number

of players on each side of the net. In an **official** game, each team has six players. Three players line up in a row in front of the net, on or near the attack lines. The other three players stand behind them, toward the back of the court. Each player stays in his or her general position during a volley. As the game goes on, the players **rotate** around the court. Each player takes a turn at every position.

The game begins when the player of one team hits or "serves" the ball across the net. Players on the opposite team use their hands, fists, or arms to hit the ball back across the net. Players are not allowed to catch, scoop, or throw the ball.

Players may hit the ball as many as three times while it is on their side of the court. If the ball touches the ground or if the players hit it too many times, the volley or "rally" is over. The other team scores a point. If the

A young player serves the ball (top left). When players use their forearms to pass the ball, it is called a "bump" (top right). If the ball touches the ground out of bounds (bottom), the rally is over.

ball touches the ground out of bounds, the team that touched the ball last loses the rally, and the other team scores a point.

Each team tries to keep the ball from touching the ground on its side of the net.

If the serving team wins a rally, it scores a point and continues serving. If the other team wins a rally, it scores a point and the right to serve, and its players rotate clockwise one position.

The first team to score 25 points wins the game. However, a team must win by 2 points. If the score reaches 25-24, play continues until one of the teams earns a 2-point lead.

In some competitions, the same two teams will play several games in a row. The team that wins two out of three games (or three out of five games) wins the match.

In the United States, **recreational** players and younger players often use a different scoring method called "sideout scoring." If the serving team wins a rally, it scores a point and continues serving. If the serving team loses a rally, the other team gets a turn to serve, but no point is scored. When sideout scoring is used, teams usually play only to 15 points.

Volleyball can be played in a park, on the beach, or in a

gymnasium. No uniforms or special equipment are needed. Some people choose to play barefoot, in shorts and T-shirts. Others wear jeans and sneakers.

In official competitions, teams usually do have uniforms. Shorts

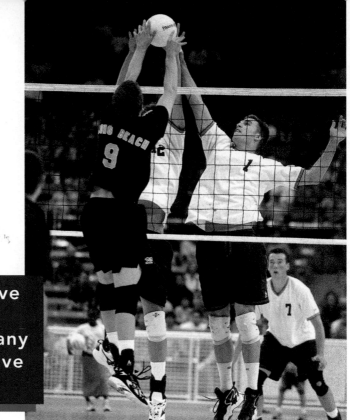

Usually, competitive volleyball players wear uniforms. Many also wear protective kneepads.

give players the freedom to move quickly. Special rubber-soled shoes help their feet grip the court. Many players wear kneepads to protect their knees from scrapes and bruises.

Having a Ball

When William Morgan invented volleyball, he borrowed equipment from several other sports. He took the net from tennis and gave players a basketball to hit over it. Basketballs were too heavy, however. They hurt the players' arms and hands. So Morgan took the inner lining (or bladder) out of the basketball and used it by itself. This ball was too light! A sporting-goods company designed a soft, medium-sized ball just for volleyball players. This type of ball is still used today.

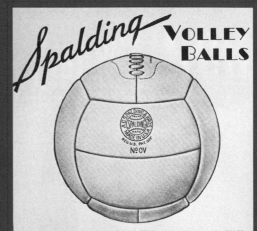

A volleyball ad from the 1920s

The Skills

A volleyball game begins with a serve. The right, back-row player stands behind the end line to serve the ball up into the air and across the net. On the other side of the net, the first player to touch the ball makes a "pass." With this shot, the player

A young player passing the ball to a teammate

keeps the ball off the ground and sends it to a teammate.

25

The next player hits the ball toward a third teammate at the net. This hit is called a "set," because it sets the ball

A college player setting the ball for a teammate

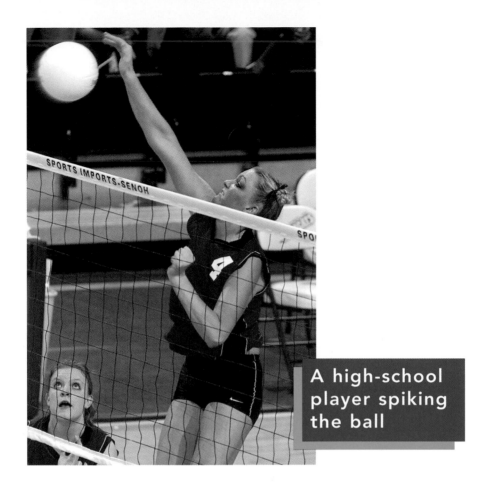

up for the third and final shot. The player at the net leaps into the air and strikes the ball as it comes down toward the net. With this "spike," the

Three players
attempting to
block a shot

player tries to hit the ball so hard that it falls straight to the ground on the other side of the net. Then the **opponents** won't be able to hit it back.

When one or more front-row opponents see a player preparing to spike the ball, they leap into the air and attempt to "block" the shot—to keep it from coming over the net. If the ball does make it over, the defenders

A professional beach volleyball player dives to keep the ball in play.

may dive to the ground and try to hit a pass, keeping the ball in play.

These shots—pass, set, spike, and block—form a pattern that is repeated over and over again throughout the game. It takes teamwork and skill to make these shots work. The team that performs them most correctly and successfully will win the game.

The Competition

Although volleyball began as a recreational game, it has become a fast-paced, action-packed competitive sport. For beginners, there are youth leagues and junior competitions. High-school and college teams compete with other schools in local, state, and national tournaments.

The best volleyball players
in the world compete in inter-
national tournaments. They
represent their countries in

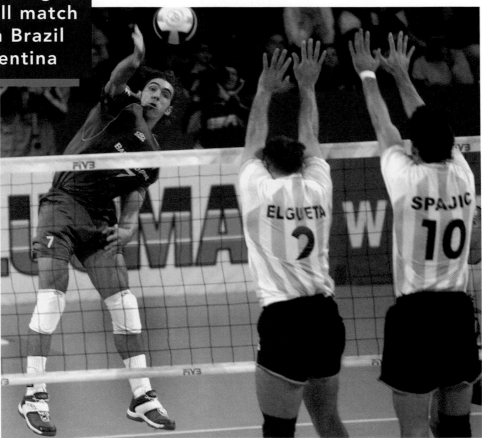

competitions for the World Cup,
the World Championships, the
Goodwill Games, and the
Olympic Summer Games.

Although volleyball was invented in the United States, the game has become extremely popular in Japan. Japan worked hard to get volleyball accepted as an official Olympic sport. The

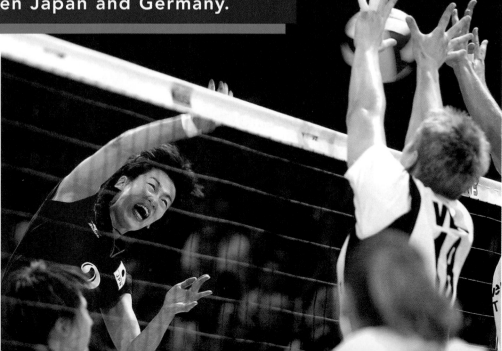

A member of the Japanese team smashes the ball during a women's World Championship match between Japan and Germany.

Japanese women's team won the first gold medal for volleyball at the Olympic Summer Games in 1964. Diving, jumping, and rolling across the court, they showed the world a brand-new way to play volleyball. People loved this athletic style of "power volleyball."

Twenty years after volleyball first appeared at the Olympics, the United States finally won medals in the sport. In 1984, the U.S. men's team took the

The U.S. men's team celebrates after winning the gold medal at the 1984 Olympic Summer Games.

gold medal in the men's competition. That same year, the U.S. women's team won a silver medal.

Beach Volleyball

Beach volleyball is much more than fun in the sun—it's serious competition! There's even a professional league. It takes a lot of strength and energy to play this fast-paced game. With only two people on each team, the players have much more court to cover. They must learn to keep their balance when the sand moves under their feet. Heat and wind may affect the players, too. Beach volleyball became an official Olympic sport in 1996.

An overhead view of beach volleyball at the 2000 Olympic Summer Games (top) and a women's professional beach volleyball game (bottom)

Making the Team

For over a hundred years, people around the world have enjoyed playing volleyball. Some people play volleyball just for fun. Some play for exercise. Others play for the thrill of competition—the excitement that comes with winning a big game.

Serious volleyball players warm up before a game with stretches (left) and exercises (above).

Serious players know that it's important to practice their skills every day. These athletes take care to stretch their muscles and warm up properly before they step onto the court. Stretching helps prevent injuries. Players do special drills—exercises that help them improve their shots. They use other exercises such as jogging, jumping rope, sit-ups, pull-ups, and push-ups to strengthen their muscles. They eat healthy foods to give them energy.

Good players listen to their coaches and learn everything they can about their sport. They work with their teammates and try to help each other. When they play that way, everybody wins!

Players react to winning a college volleyball tournament.

To Find Out More

Here are some additional resources to help you learn more about the game of volleyball:

 **Books**

Blackall, Bernie. **Volleyball.** Heinemann Library, 1998.

Jensen, Julie. **Play by Play Volleyball.** Lerner Publishing Group, 2001.

Kalman, Bobbie, and Sarah Dann. **Volleyball In Action.** Crabtree Publishing Co., 1999.

Kelly, Zach A., and David Armentrout. **Volleyball: Basics of the Game.** Rourke Corporation, 1998.

Lucas, Jeff. **Pass, Set, Crush: Volleyball Illustrated.** Euclid Northwest Publications, 1992.

Smale, David. **Volleyball.** Smart Apple Media, 1995.

Organizations and Online Sites

United States Youth Volleyball League

12501 South Isis Avenue
Hawthorne, CA 90250
http://www.usyvl.org

The mission of this non-profit organization is to "provide every child between the ages of 8-14 a chance to learn to play volleyball in a fun, safe, supervised environment."

USA Volleyball

715 S. Circle Drive
Colorado Springs, CO 80910
http://www.usavolleyball.org

USA Volleyball is the national governing body for the sport of volleyball in the United States, training players, coaches, and officials.

Volleyball Hall of Fame

444 Dwight Street
Holyoke, MA 01040
http://www.volleyhall.org

The Volleyball Hall of Fame is located in Holyoke, Massachusetts, the birthplace of volleyball. This organization commemorates and celebrates the history of the game.

Volleyball World Wide

http://www.volleyball.org

This website provides information on all aspects of the sport of volleyball, from beginner to professional levels, and from high-school competitions to the Olympics.

Important Words

boundary line that separates one place from another

competitive eager to win

drill exercise that teaches people how to do something by having them do it over and over again

fitness health and strength

missionary person sent out to convert people to his or her religion

official authorized, approved

opponents people who compete against you in a contest or game

recreational referring to a game or activity that people enjoy in their spare time

rotate to take turns in a specific order

tournaments series of games or contests in which teams compete to win championships

Index

Meet the Author

Christin Ditchfield is the author of more than twenty books for children, including nine True Books on sports. A former elementary-school teacher, she is now a freelance writer, conference speaker, and host of the nationally syndicated radio program "Take It To Heart!" Ms. Ditchfield makes her home in Sarasota, Florida.

Photographs © 2003: AllSport USA/Getty Images: 40 right (Brian Bahr), 1 (Al Bello), 37 (Bruce Hazelton), 26 (Ken Levine), 13 (Darren McNamara), 38 bottom (Doug Pensinger), 38 top (Mike Powell), 17 center (Ezra Shaw); AP/Wide World Photos: 27 (Deborah Cannon), 34 (Eduardo Di Baia), 30 (Gert Eggenberger), 23 top (Douglas Engle), 43 (Dean Hoffmeyer/Richmond Times-Dispatch), 35 (Martin Meissner), 40 left (Jens Meyer), 28, 42 (Eraldo Peres), 17 right (Mark J. Terrill), 2 (Rodney White); Corbis Images: 11 (Christophe Loviny), 18 (Roy Morsch), 21 (Phil Schermeister); NCAA Photos/Rich Clarkson and Associates, LLC: 22 (Hans Gutknecht), cover (Chas Hendrickson); U.S. Youth Volleyball League/Craig T. Mathew: 4, 17 left, 25, 33; Volleyball Hall of Fame: 23 bottom, 7 right, 7 left, 9.